A CENTURY *of*
LANCASHIRE

ELECTRIC CAR, CROSSING SHIP CANAL TO WIDNES.

Bootle, 1932. Schools have always put on excellent productions of plays, concerts and other forms of entertainment for parents and the local community. This composite photograph was taken in 1932 when the pupils of Roberts Council School in Bootle put on a performance.

A CENTURY *of* LANCASHIRE

CHRIS MAKEPEACE

SUTTON PUBLISHING

First published in the United Kingdom in 2000 by
Sutton Publishing Limited · Phoenix Mill
Thrupp · Stroud · Gloucestershire · GL5 2BU

Paperback edition first published in 2004

British Library Cataloguing in Publication Data
A catalogue record for this book is available from the British Library.

ISBN 0-7509-3881-1

Front endpaper: Blackpool, *c.* 1930. Although this postcard is not dated, the photograph cannot have been taken earlier than 1929 as the big wheel, which was a feature close to the Tower, was not demolished until November 1928, leaving the Tower as a landmark on its own.

Back endpaper: Accrington, 2000. Pedestrianisation has been an important part of improving the centre of many towns and cities in Lancashire in the latter half of the twentieth century. This photograph shows the pedestrianised centre of Accrington, close to the market, where seats have been placed and raised beds for flowers add a splash of colour to the scene. The whole scene is dominated by Cannon Street Baptist Chapel, described by Pevsner as 'more like the parish church of the town than St James'. The church, designed by George Baines, was completed in 1874 at a cost of £15,671. The stone of the buildings fronting Blackburn Road contrasts with the more recent buildings lining the road to the market.

Half title page: Widnes, 1908. Until 1905, it was necessary for road vehicles wanting to cross the River Mersey between Runcorn and Widnes to go via Warrington. Proposals for a road bridge had been made by Telford, but nothing was done until 1900 when an Act of Parliament was passed allowing the construction of a transporter bridge between the two towns. The Runcorn–Widnes Transporter Bridge continued in use until its replacement by a high level bridge in 1961.

Title page: Darwen, *c.* 1911. During the late eighteenth century, cotton replaced wool as the main fibre produced in Lancashire. Throughout Lancashire, and especially east Lancashire, cotton mills were a common part of townscapes. Many employees in the mills were girls and women, as this photograph of weavers from Moss Bridge Mill at Darwen shows. Clearly visible are looms and the line shafting which provided the power to the looms. The decorations may have celebrated the coronation of George V in 1911.

Typeset in 11/14pt Photina.
Typesetting and origination by
Sutton Publishing Limited.
Printed in Great Britain by
J.H. Haynes & Co. Ltd, Sparkford.

Contents

Barrow-in-Furness, c. 1918. These women are making the envelopes which contained the gas that kept airships afloat. Used as barrage balloons, they and observation balloons were highly inflammable as the gas used was hydrogen. The skill these women developed became important when it came to making them for commercial airships after the war.

Foreword

BY LORD SHUTTLEWORTH

I am delighted to have been invited to write a foreword to this excellent record of Lancashire.

I come from a family lucky enough to have lived in the county of Lancashire for many hundreds of years. Records show that my ancestors were at Gawthorpe Hall near Padham from at least the fourteenth century. I say this not from any sense of self-importance – for I dare say there are many families who could say the same, but for whom the records do not exist – but because it emphasises that the tradition of our county is long and proud. Despite many changes, both of fortune and of boundaries, there has been much consistency, not least in the fortitude, resilience and determination of Lancastrians.

This is important when we look at the twentieth century through Chris Makepeace's valuable record. As he hints in his introduction, it would be possible to conclude that it was a century of decline for Lancashire, in which all the successes of the nineteenth century which put the county at the industrial heart of nation and of empire, were unravelled as jobs, indeed whole industries, disappeared. And all against the grim backcloth of human destruction in two world wars.

However, putting the twentieth century into a longer historical context could easily lead to the view that Lancashire always bounces back. Physical regeneration, particularly in the last two decades, is much in evidence. We have modern businesses, full of state of the art technology, expertise and management. Even the space and tranquillity of the large rural parts of our county may prove to be an economic asset as the south becomes ever more crowded and busy.

Chris Makepeace's book is a splendid contribution to Lancashire's story, as a matter of record, but I hope it will encourage us to look forward too, in the knowledge that our county's story has many chapters yet to run.

Lord Shuttleworth
Lord Lieutenant of Lancashire

Post Office, Preston, 2000. One of the many splendid buildings that grace the modern centre of Preston.

Britain: A Century of Change

Two women encumbered with gas masks go about their daily tasks during the early days of the war. (*Hulton Getty Picture Collection*)

The sixty years ending in 1900 were a period of huge trans-formation for Britain. Railway stations, post-and-telegraph offices, police and fire stations, gasworks and gasometers, new livestock markets and covered markets, schools, churches, football grounds, hospitals and asylums, water pumping stations and sewerage plants totally altered the urban scene, and the country's population tripled with more than seven out of ten people being born in or moving to the towns. The century that followed, leading up to the Millennium's end in 2000, was to be a period of even greater change.

When Queen Victoria died in 1901, she was measured for her coffin by her grandson Kaiser Wilhelm, the London prostitutes put on black mourning and the blinds came down in the villas and terraces spreading out from the old town centres. These centres were reachable by train and tram, by the new bicycles and still newer motor cars, were connected by the new telephone, and lit by gas or even electricity. The shops may have been full of British-made cotton and woollen clothing but the grocers and butchers were selling cheap Danish bacon, Argentinian beef, Australasian mutton and tinned or dried fish and fruit from Canada, California and South Africa. Most of these goods were carried in British-built-and-crewed ships burning Welsh steam coal.

As the first decade moved on, the Open Spaces Act meant more parks, bowling greens and cricket pitches. The First World War transformed the place of women, as they took over many men's jobs. Its other legacies were the war memorials which joined the statues of Victorian worthies in main squares round the land. After 1918 death duties and higher taxation bit hard, and a quarter of England changed hands in the space of only a few years.

The multiple shop – the chain store – appeared in the high street: Sainsburys, Maypole, Lipton's, Home & Colonial, the Fifty Shilling Tailor, Burton, Boots, W.H. Smith. The shopper was spoilt for choice, attracted by the brash fascias and advertising hoardings for national brands like Bovril, Pears Soap, and Ovaltine. Many new buildings began to be seen, such as garages, motor showrooms, picture palaces (cinemas), 'palais de dance', and ribbons of 'semis' stretched along the roads and new bypasses and onto the new estates nudging the green belts.

During the 1920s cars became more reliable and sophisticated as well as commonplace, with developments like the electric self-starter making them easier for women to drive. Who wanted to turn a crank handle in the new short skirt? This was, indeed, the electric age as much as the motor era. Trolley buses, electric trams and trains extended mass transport and electric light replaced gas in the street and the home, which itself was groomed by the vacuum cleaner.

A major jolt to the march onward and upward was administered by the Great Depression of the early 1930s. The older British industries –

textiles, shipbuilding, iron, steel, coal – were already under pressure from foreign competition when this worldwide slump arrived. Luckily there were new diversions to alleviate the misery. The 'talkies' arrived in the cinemas; more and more radios and gramophones were to be found in people's homes; there were new women's magazines, with fashion, cookery tips and problem pages; football pools; the flying feats of women pilots like Amy Johnson; the Loch Ness Monster; cheap chocolate and the drama of Edward VIII's abdication.

Things were looking up again by 1936 and new light industry was booming in the Home Counties as factories struggled to keep up with the demand for radios, radiograms, cars and electronic goods, including the first television sets. The threat from Hitler's Germany meant rearmament, particularly of the airforce, which stimulated aircraft and aero engine firms. If you were lucky and lived in the south, there was good money to be earned. A semi-detached house cost £450, a Morris Cowley £150. People may have smoked like chimneys but life expectancy, since 1918, was up by 15 years while the birth rate had almost halved.

In some ways it is the little memories that seem to linger longest from the Second World War: the kerbs painted white to show up in the

A W.H. Smith shop front in Beaconsfield, 1922.

blackout, the rattle of ack-ack shrapnel on roof tiles, sparrows killed by bomb blast. The biggest damage, apart from London, was in the south-west (Plymouth, Bristol) and the Midlands (Coventry, Birmingham). Postwar reconstruction was rooted in the Beveridge Report which set out the expectations for the Welfare State. This, together with the nationalisation of the Bank of England, coal, gas, electricity and the railways, formed the programme of the Labour government in 1945.

Children collecting aluminium to help the war effort, London, 1940s. (*IWM*)

Times were hard in the late 1940s, with rationing even more stringent than during the war. Yet this was, as has been said, 'an innocent and well-behaved era'. The first let-up came in 1951 with the Festival of Britain and there was another fillip in 1953 from the Coronation, which incidentally gave a huge boost to the spread of TV. By 1954 leisure motoring had been resumed but the Comet – Britain's best hope for taking on the American aviation industry – suffered a series of mysterious crashes. The Suez debacle of 1956 was followed by an acceleration in the withdrawal from Empire, which had begun in 1947 with the Independence of India. Consumerism was truly born with the advent of commercial TV and most homes soon boasted washing machines, fridges, electric irons and fires.

A street party to celebrate the Queen's Coronation, June 1953. (*Hulton Getty Picture Collection*)

The *Lady Chatterley* obscenity trial in 1960 was something of a straw in the wind for what was to follow in that decade. A collective loss of inhibition seemed to sweep the land, as the Beatles and the Rolling Stones transformed popular music, and retailing, cinema and the theatre were revolutionised. Designers, hair-dressers, photographers and models moved into places vacated by an Establishment put to flight by the new breed of satirists spawned by *Beyond the Fringe* and *Private Eye*.

In the 1970s Britain seems to have suffered a prolonged hangover after the excesses of the previous decade. Ulster, inflation and union troubles were not made up for by entry into the EEC, North Sea Oil, Women's Lib or, indeed, Punk Rock. Mrs Thatcher applied the corrective in the 1980s, as the country moved more and more from its old manufacturing base over to providing services, consulting, advertising, and expertise in the 'invisible' market of high finance or in IT.

The post-1945 townscape has seen changes to match those in the worlds of work, entertainment and politics. In 1952 the Clean Air Act served notice on smogs and pea-souper fogs, smuts and blackened buildings, forcing people to stop burning coal and go over to smokeless sources of heat and energy. In the same decade some of the best urban building took place in the 'new towns' like Basildon, Crawley, Stevenage and Harlow. Elsewhere open warfare was declared on slums and what was labelled inadequate, cramped, back-to-back, two-up, two-down, housing. The new 'machine for living in' was a flat in a high-rise block. The architects and planners who promoted these were in league with the traffic engineers, determined to keep the motor car moving whatever the price in multi-storey car parks, meters, traffic wardens and ring roads. The old pollutant, coal smoke, was replaced by petrol and diesel exhaust, and traffic noise.

Fast food was no longer only a pork pie in a pub or fish-and-chips. There were Indian curry houses, Chinese take-aways and American-style hamburgers, while the drinker could get away from beer in a wine bar. Under the impact of television

Punk rockers demonstrate their anarchic style during the 1970s. (*Barnaby's Picture Library*)

the big Gaumonts and Odeons closed or were rebuilt as multi-screen cinemas, while the palais de dance gave way to discos and clubs.

From the late 1960s the introduction of listed buildings and conservation areas, together with the growth of preservation societies, put a brake on 'comprehensive redevelopment'. The end of the century and the start of the Third Millennium see new challenges to the health of towns and the wellbeing of the nine out of ten people who now live urban lives. The fight is on to prevent town centres from dying, as patterns of housing and shopping change, and edge-of-town supermarkets exercise the attractions of one-stop shopping. But as banks and department stores close, following the haberdashers, greengrocers, butchers and ironmongers, there are signs of new growth such as farmers' markets, and corner stores acting as pick-up points where customers collect shopping ordered on-line from web sites.

Futurologists tell us that we are in stage two of the consumer revolution: a shift from mass consumption to mass customisation driven by a

Millennium celebrations over the Thames at Westminster, New Year's Eve, 1999. (*Barnaby's Picture Library*)

desire to have things that fit us and our particular lifestyle exactly, and for better service. This must offer hope for small city-centre shop premises, as must the continued attraction of physical shopping, browsing and being part of a crowd: in a word, 'shoppertainment'. Another hopeful trend for towns is the growth in the number of young people postponing marriage and looking to live independently, alone, where there is a buzz, in 'swinging single cities'. Theirs is a 'flats-and-cafés' lifestyle, in contrast to the 'family suburbs', and certainly fits in with government's aim of building 60 per cent of the huge amount of new housing needed on 'brown' sites, recycled urban land. There looks to be plenty of life in the British town yet.

Lancashire: An Introduction

If a map of Lancashire from 1901 is compared with one from 1999, it will appear that the area covered by the County of Lancashire has been considerably reduced. In administrative terms, this is correct as the reorganisation of local government in 1974 resulted in the Furness area becoming part of Cumbria, south-east Lancashire formed part of Greater Manchester, Warrington was transferred to Cheshire and the area around Liverpool became part of Merseyside. More recently, both Blackburn and Blackpool have become unitary authorities and are no longer part of the area administered by Lancashire County Council. However, in spite of these changes in administrative boundaries, many of those who were born in the area covered by Lancashire as it was until 1974 still regard themselves as Lancastrians. As John Walton comments in the introduction to his book *Lancashire: a social history 1558–1939*, these people are proud of the history of the county and its traditions. Whatever politicians and administrators do to boundaries, they find it difficult to alter the traditional allegiances. What is left of the Lancashire of 1901 was aptly summed up by Nicholas Pevsner when he gave the second volume *Buildings of England: North Lancashire* the sub-title 'The Rural North', which is a very true description. Apart from Preston and the surrounding area, Lancaster, parts of north-east Lancashire and the coast, the remainder of the county is rural in nature with the sparsely populated Pennine moors on the east and an agricultural landscape with villages on the plain.

For the purposes of this book on Lancashire in the twentieth century, I have used the traditional boundaries of the county which means that towns like Barrow-in-Furness, Warrington, Southport, Wigan, Bolton, Bury, Rochdale and Oldham as well as Preston, Nelson, Colne, Lancaster and Fleetwood have been included.

Lancashire is a county of contrasts. In the east there are the bleak uplands of the Pennines, with more sheep than people, while only a few miles away are the teeming industrial towns of East Lancashire and what is now Greater Manchester. Travelling westwards, there are the agricultural belts between the towns and industrial centres of East Lancashire and towns like Preston, Lancaster, Chorley and Warrington in the central section of the county. Further westwards is the coast, with its holiday resorts of Southport, St Anne's, Blackpool, Fleetwood and Morecombe, while at the entrance of the Rivers Mersey, Ribble, Wyre and Lune there are port facilities, although only a shadow of their nineteenth-century glory.

Walton points out in his book that Lancashire in the sixteenth century was at the very edge of England, a place to be visited only when necessary. He suggests that today it is a place which is passed through, or over and implies that the county has reverted back to something like its former position. However, in the latter half of the eighteenth and nineteenth centuries, things were very different. Lancashire was the centre of the cotton textile industry, exports of which made a very significant contribution to the country's balance of payments. The industrial part of Lancashire was not solely reliant on cotton for its wealth and prosperity. There was also an important engineering industry making a range of goods including textile machines, ships and railway engines. Although many of the towns and cities of Lancashire were dominated by the mill or factory chimney, there were others where the dominant structure was the pit head gear of the local coal mines. Lancashire is situated on an important coalfield, stretching from Nelson and Colne in the north-east of the county, to Wigan and St Helens in the west, Milnrow and Oldham in the south-east and the River Mersey in the south. It was Lancashire coal which fuelled the boilers which drove the engines which powered the machinery that made Lancashire such an important economic force in the nineteenth century. So it remained until the First World War.

The end of the First World War saw a very different situation unfold. A short-lived boom in the cotton industry turned into a slump and then depression. Unemployment in the cotton industry rose as former competitors abroad began to produce cheaper cotton cloth on more modern machinery, which had been made and exported from Lancashire. Although some mill owners had been prepared to modernise before the First World War, many were content to continue to use machines that had served them well for decades. The loss of overseas markets was a disaster for Lancashire. Unemployment among workers in some of the cotton districts was between 45 per cent and 50 per cent in the 1930s. The decline in the cotton industry had an effect on other industries as well. Unemployed people do not have money to spend and firms that are cutting costs might not buy more equipment, and so the spiral gathers pace and recession becomes depression and slump. It was only when the clouds of war began to gather from the mid-1930s and the government began a rearmament programme that things started to improve.

However, not all parts of Lancashire suffered from these very high levels of unemployment. There were areas where new industry was beginning to make an impression. For example, between 1912 and 1929, Trafford Park in Stretford was the home of Ford in the United Kingdom while the Vulcan Works at Southport turned out hand-made motor cars, and at Leyland a factory was built to produce lorries and buses. Motorised vehicles increasingly began to replace horse drawn ones during the 1920s and 1930s. However, by the outbreak of the Second World War, car production had ceased in Lancashire as modern production-line techniques were introduced by firms like Ford and Morris in different parts of the country. It was not to return to Lancashire until the 1960s when Ford opened a new plant at Halewood near Liverpool. Firms like Leyland and Crossleys survived as they were producing goods vehicles and buses.

Although new forms of engineering developed, such as the aircraft industry and electrical engineering, the old heavy engineering of Lancashire did not fully recover from the 1930s. The war helped many firms to survive, but after the war, many gradually faded away and closed down. Ship building disappeared except at Barrow, locomotive building ceased at Horwich and Manchester, and general engineering ceased in many towns. Even the mining industry contracted after the war so that by the end of the century there were no deep mines operating in the county. New industry has made its appearance, but it does not employ the numbers that the old industries did before 1914.

To many people outside Lancashire, the county is associated with holidays. Every year until the 1960s, millions of people from all parts of England, Wales, Scotland and Ireland made their way to the seaside resorts of Lancashire for their annual holidays. Until after the Second World War, people had to save to go away as there were no paid holidays, but after the war, with the introduction of paid holidays, numbers continued to increase until the foreign holiday market began to make inroads. On summer Saturdays, the railways between the coast and places like Wigan, Preston and Lancaster were busy not only with normal train services, but also with the vast number of holiday extras which ran from various towns and cities. In addition, there were sometimes weekday excursions from areas in their annual holiday fortnights. Today, the number of holiday trains is virtually nil; people travel by car to the seaside, creating traffic congestion in the towns.

The increasing use of the motor car also saw Lancashire in the forefront of motorway construction, with two important sections being opened in the late 1950s and early 1960s – the Stretford–Eccles bypass, now part of the M60, and the Preston bypass, now part of the M6. Both these bypasses resulted in new structures being built to carry the roads over the Manchester Ship Canal and across river valleys. Structures such as the Thelwall Viaduct and the Barton High Level Bridge have become symbols of the motorway age as much as the motorways themselves. It should also be remembered that it was in Lancashire that one of the earliest dual carriageway roads was constructed – the East Lancashire Road (A580), linking Manchester and Liverpool, bypassing Warrington and St Helens. This speeded up the road journey between the two cities considerably, as all towns and villages along its route were bypassed. However, traffic problems remained at either end, as the road did not continue right into the centres of either city.

Lancashire was, in the nineteenth century, the place where the intercity railway came into existence with the building of the Liverpool and Manchester Railway. In the twentieth century, early trials were made using electricity to power trains on the Holcombe Brook branch and later between Manchester and Bury, Liverpool and Southport. In the post-war modernisation of the railways, it was from Manchester and Liverpool that the first electric trains ran, only as far as Crewe initially, but eventually to London.

International transport has always been important in Lancashire. During the nineteenth century, the docks at Liverpool were where raw materials were imported and finished products shipped overseas. Today, the newer docks in Liverpool are at Seaforth rather than in the centre of the town. Even so, they remain important import and export points for the United Kingdom, although passenger traffic, which saw so many people leave for North America, no longer exists. The Princes Landing Stage no longer witnesses the Cunard or Canadian Pacific liners leaving Liverpool for Canada and America. The Albert Dock has become a heritage and cultural centre attracting thousands of visitors each year.

It is not only the docks that have become involved in the preservation of the past. At Carnforth and Bury, there are thriving railway museums where the leviathans of the steam age on the railways can still be seen operating. Even the textile industry has become part of the Lancashire heritage tradition with Queen Street Mills in Burnley, Helmshaw Mill in Rossendale and the steam engine at Ellen Road Mill, Milnrow all preserved so that present and future generations can see the type of machinery that existed in Lancashire's factories and mills.

To try to cover every town and village in a book like this is virtually impossible. So much material has survived for each period that selections have to be made. It is not only street scenes that have to be included, but also events, people's recreational activities and industry. An attempt has been made to reflect the diversity of land and townscapes in the county, the diversity of its industry and how people spent some of their growing leisure time. Needless to say, some areas have been excluded not because they were unimportant, but because of a lack of space. It is hoped that overall the book paints a picture of the changing face of an area traditionally known as the 'Red Rose County' of Lancashire.

Edwardian Lancashire

Lancaster, c. 1900. Once the visitor left the main streets, he or she plunged into a world of narrow, overcrowded streets where people lived and worked, a complete contrast to the fine buildings that were to be found only a few yards away. This photograph shows China Lane, which linked Church Street with Market Street and was only a short distance from Lancaster Castle and prison.

Morecambe *c.* 1914. Morecambe, Lancashire's most northerly holiday resort, developed as a holiday resort during the last two decades of the nineteenth century. The town regarded itself as a rival to Blackpool and even started to build a tower, which was never completed, and had its own illuminations. The resort, with its wide promenade shown here, was popular with people from the woollen towns of West Yorkshire. The clock tower was given to the town by John Robert Birkett, mayor between 1903 and 1907. Horse trams continued to operate in Morecambe until 1926 when they were finally abolished, although not without opposition.

Southport, *c.* 1910. This tree-lined boulevard is Lord Street which had shops and the Scarsbrick Hotel on the seaward side and the Town Hall, Cambridge Hall, library, hotels and shops on the other. In front of the Town Hall were the Memorial Gardens, to which a bandstand was later added. The shops in 1910 included costumiers, milliners and jewellers as well as those selling souvenirs.

Longridge, *c.* 1905. About six miles north east of Preston is the village of Longridge which, it was proposed in 1846, would be served by a railway linking Fleetwood, Preston Clitheroe and Blackburn. However, the line, which got no further than Longridge, was opened in November 1848 although trains did not run into the main station at Preston until 1885. The line closed for passenger traffic in 1930, the victim of bus competition. This is the main street in the village, climbing up out of the Ribble Valley, and shows the level crossing, which cannot have been very busy as the train service was not at all frequent.

St Helens, *c.* 1910. Lancashire is not all an industrial landscape as this picture of Moss Bank near St Helens shows. Farming was an important industry in many parts of the county, especially in the areas between the large towns and cities as there was always a demand for fresh milk, vegetables and meat. The only sign of anything 'modern' in the picture are the telephone poles and wires in a landscape which would have hardly changed over several centuries.

Preston, *c.* 1905. At the beginning of the twentieth century, there were three railway bridges crossing the River Ribble in the centre of Preston. This one was built between 1835 and 1838 to carry the North Union Railway over the river into Preston. At the time, various companies were competing to reach Preston, all of them wanting their own access and stations. This explains why new bridges were built rather than enlarging and sharing the existing one.

Sabden, *c.* 1910. The village of Sabden like many other villages and small towns in the Ribble Valley owes much of its prosperity to the textile industry. Sabden was large enough to have its own church by 1846. Behind the village rises the bleak Pennine hills where the main farming activity is the rearing of sheep.

Lancaster, *c.* 1910. Williamson Park was given to the city of Lancaster in 1881 by James Williamson, a linoleum manufacturer. Since 1910 the park has been dominated by the Ashton Memorial, given by Lord Ashton (formerly James Williamson) in memory, so the story goes, of his second wife. John Champness, in *Lancashire's architectural heritage* says, however, that it was erected in memory of the whole family. The Memorial is 150 feet high and was designed by Sir John Belcher. Nicholas Pevsner described it as 'the grandest monument in England' in his book on the buildings of North Lancashire. The Memorial, which cost £87,000, is not only a landmark in Lancaster but is clearly visible to traffic using the near-by M6.

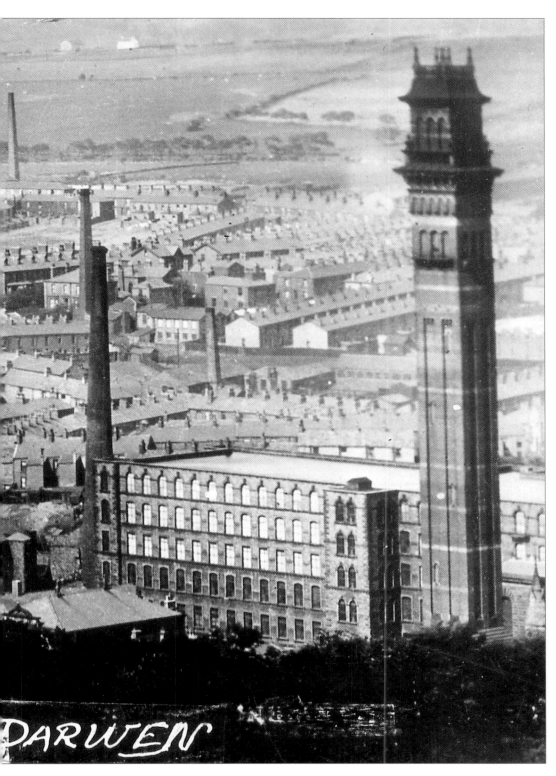

Darwen, *c.* 1910. This picture shows the town of Darwen with its mills and rows of terraced housing for those who worked in the mills. Around the time this picture was taken, Darwen boasted that it had 57 weaving mills with 32,000 looms and 8 spinning mills with 300,000 spindles. Its population in 1911 was given as 40,398, many of whom worked in the mills or paper works. The spectacular chimney on the right is that of India Mill, which was built between 1859 and 1867 and rises to over 300 feet.

Narrowgates in Pendle, *c.* 1904. The caption on this picture reads 'Narrowgates in Pendle', but where exactly Narrowgates was is not clear. There is a 'Higher Narrowgates' near Newchurch. Perhaps the title is a shortened version of this. The buildings in the background appear to be industrial with a factory chimney, but it is not possible to identify what was produced here. To the right of the two storeyed building there is a bridge that crosses a stream or the Leeds–Liverpool Canal, which went via north-east Lancashire into Yorkshire.

Warrington, 1914. This photograph shows Bridge Street in the centre of Warrington, looking towards Sankey Street, Horse Market Street and Buttermarket Street. Bridge Street got its name from the fact that it led from the town centre to the oldest crossing point of the River Mersey, Warrington Bridge. There has been a bridge at this point since about 1285 when there is evidence of tolls being collected on goods passing over the bridge. Bridge Street was widened in the late nineteenth century to reduce congestion although the bridge itself was not rebuilt until the second decade of the twentieth century.

Barrow-in-Furness, *c*. 1914. View of Abbey Road in Barrow taken just before the outbreak of war in 1914 looking towards Ramsden Square. The impressive building on the right is the Technical School, designed by Woodhouse and Willoughby and completed in 1900, beyond which is the Ramsden Hall. Further along, the building wth the cupola, marked on a contemporary map as 'Club and Institute', dates from 1870–1 and was designed by H.A. Darbishire. The church on the edge of the picture is Christ Church.

Blackpool, 1911. Although many people see the sea at Blackpool in a benign mood, it can be exceptionally rough and do serious damage to the promenade and sea defences, causing problems not only for pedestrians, but also for trams.

Sawley Abbey, *c*. 1900. The Cistercian Abbey of Sawley in the Ribble Valley near Clitheroe, was founded by monks from Northumberland in 1148. It was never a large, rich abbey, had only a few monks and was overshadowed by the nearby Whalley Abbey. Sawley Abbey was closed down in 1536 and gradually left to decay. Local people used the stone for building so that, by the early twentieth century, all that remained were a few walls overgrown with vegetation. However, even these remains were of interest to visitors who visited the area. The remains have now been conserved and members of the public are able to visit the site.

Bolton, *c*. 1901. This is perhaps 'Hulton Lane Ends', where four roads meet. They lead to Bolton, Liverpool, Chorley and Manchester. 'The Little Wooden Hut' was a newsagents that would have served not only those who lived locally, but also a wide area which consisted of a few houses and farms. The newspaper headline refers to a breach of a local canal and racing news.

Urmston, *c.* 1912. Urmston Station was opened by the Cheshire Lines Committee in 1873. During the late nineteenth and early twentieth centuries, Urmston became one of the areas fashionable commuter towns with its frequent and reliable services into Manchester. Like all stations at this time, Urmston had its own bookstall.

Excursion Platform.

Morecambe, *c.* 1905. Until the railway arrived, there was little more than a village, Poulton-le-Sands, here. Like many seaside towns, there were special platforms which were used to handle the large number of excursion and holiday trains that descended on the town during the summer months. This illustrations gives some impression of the numbers who came to Morecambe by train in the early twentieth century.

STATION N°. 5, ROCHDALE.   T. PINDER. PHOTO.

Rochdale, 1913. Rochdale Station opened in 1839 and was one of the original stations on the Manchester and Leeds Railway line to Yorkshire. The station at that time lay about a ¼ mile east of the present station, which was built in 1889. The station was also the terminus of the line from Manchester to Oldham via Royton which was completed at the end of 1863 for passengers.

Carnforth, *c*. 1910. The original station was opened in 1846 by the London and North Western Railway, and replaced in 1864 by a new station shared with the Furness Railway. Sixteen years later, the station was replaced by one shared by these two companies and the Midland Railway. As a result, it was possible to change at Carnforth for Barrow-in-Furness, the Cumbrian coast, Lancashire, the Midlands, Scotland and areas east of the Pennines.

Middleton, *c*. 1914. Middleton was by-passed when the railway between Manchester and Rochdale was built. Although plans were made for a line to be constructed to link the town with the main line, nothing was done until 1854 when the construction of a branch line to the town was authorised. The line was opened in 1857 with Middleton Station having just a single platform. This was not convenient so, in 1885, a second platform was constructed. The station survived until 1964 when it was closed after years of under use reflecting the fact that buses were more convenient than the train over relatively short distances.

Ormskirk, *c*. 1902. The station was opened in 1849 by the Liverpool, Preston and Ormskirk Railway, which was eventually absorbed by the East Lancashire Railway, which became part of the Lancashire and Yorkshire Railway. The route provided a direct link between Liverpool and Preston and reduced the time taken to travel between these two towns.

Rochdale, 1905. Before the introduction of electric trams, both horse and steam power was used to haul tram cars which could carry as many as forty passengers at speeds of up to 7 miles per hour. In urban areas, it was the horse tram which predominated. This photograph shows the last journey of a steam tram between Rochdale and Littleborough.

Littleborough, 1905. The arrival of the first electric tram brought the children out to see this new form of transport which was much quieter than the old steam trams. As with many of the openings of electric tramways, the first tram always carried a number of local dignitaries, eager to be shown as supporters of progress. The electric trams in Rochdale were eventually replaced by motor buses in 1932.

Knott End, *c.* 1907. To get between Fleetwood on the south side of the River Wyre and Knott End on the north side of the river involved a long train journey to Preston and then to Garstang or taking the ferry across the river. In the background is Fleetwood, with the North Euston Hotel and the Pharos lighthouse visible.

Failsworth, *c.* 1907. The Rochdale Canal was completed in 1804 and shortened the distance between Liverpool and Hull. To complete the journey across the Pennines involved passing through ninety-two locks and under numerous bridges like this one at Failsworth, east of Manchester.

Worsley, *c.* 1904. The village of Worsley was originally a mining village associated with the coal mines owned by the Duke of Bridgewater who, in the mid-eighteenth century, built the Bridgewater Canal to transport coal to Manchester. Court House, the mock black and white building, was erected in the nineteenth century. Several of the boats seen here on the canal were used to carry coal into Manchester. The small bridge is known as the 'ABC Bridge' because it has 26 boards creating the walkway. In the background are some of the industrial buildings associated with the local pits.

Trafford Park, *c.* 1912. In 1911 the Ford Company of America opened its factory in Trafford Park to manufacture motor cars for the UK market. The firm planned to produce 7,500 cars a year but in the first year only 1,485 were built which had risen to 6,139 a year by the end of 1913. During 1914, mass production was introduced which allowed between seven and twenty-one cars to be produced every hour. This factory produced not only Model T cars, but also touring and saloon cars and small vans. Ford stayed at Trafford Park until 1931 when it was tempted to Dagenham by the offer of better grants and room to expand.

Crossens, *c.* 1910. In 1898 two brothers, Joseph and Thomas Hampson, started a small factory to make 'horseless carriages', or motor cars. The new firm was so successful that in 1907 they moved to a new factory at Crossens where they employed 700 men, making an average of twenty hand-made cars per week.

Winding Room.

Weaving Sl

LANCASHIRE INDU

Warehouse.

Five different aspects of the Lancashire cotton industry, *c.* 1910. The only aspects of the production processes that appear to be missing are spinning, bleaching and dyeing, which would have been carried out on different sites from the manufacture of the yarn and the cloth.

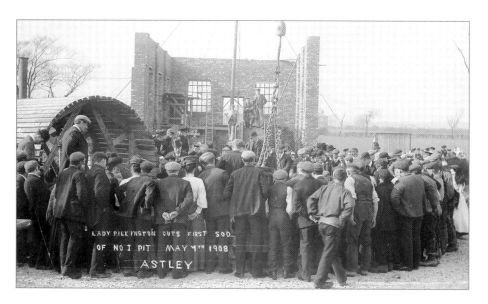

Astley Green, 1908. Although Lancashire is associated with cotton, there was also an important and profitable mining industry. In 1908, a new pit was sunk at Astley by Clifton and Kearsley Coal Company Limited. This photograph was taken when Lady Pilkington cut the first sod at Astley Colliery in 1908, which was fully operational by 1913.

Haydock, *c.* 1905. This area had a number of important collieries in the nineteenth and twentieth centuries and several serious accidents resulted in a heavy loss of life. This picture shows another side of mining which is often overlooked, supporting local events. The immaculately groomed horse, together with the highly polished horse brasses, and smartly dressed men, appear to be ready to take part either in a traditional May Day Parade of working horses or a local carnival.

Haydock, *c.* 1910. Although women and girls were not employed underground in the coal mines of Lancashire, they were employed on the surface in sorting the coal which the miners had sent up. The close-fitting shawls around the head were an attempt to prevent their hair getting too dirty in what was a very dirty operation.

Leigh, 1911. The years 1911 and 1912 were notable for the number of strikes which occurred in many parts of Lancashire. In order to maintain law and order and ensure that supplies got through to the town, soldiers were stationed in the town. Sitting on the wall of the local police station are members of the 16th Lancers, presumably awaiting their instructions.

Rochdale, 1912. The miners' strike of 1911 had serious repercussions not only for industry, but also for families who relied on coal for heating and cooking. These boys appear to be taking the coke home in sacks either for their parents or for a neighbour.

Littleborough, *c.* 1902–7. This photograph was taken on the Rochdale Canal at Littleborough where members of the Holy Trinity church school were embarking on a day trip either towards Rochdale or Summit and Todmorden. The barge which they are using would normally have carried goods and have been towed by another vessel, which may be the one on the extreme left of the picture.

Rainford, 1906. Another treat for school children, but this time at Rainford. The local colliery brass band is leading the procession, followed by a banner. Behind the banner come the children from the company's school, in their best clothes, led by their teachers.

The First World War

Horwich, *c.* 1925. When the First World War ended, every town and community erected memorials to those who were killed. Some were very plain, especially those in churches, schools and places of work, but those erected by local authorities tended to be more elaborate. This memorial was erected by the management of Horwich Locomotive Works and names all those who worked there that died during the war, together with their rank.

Accrington, 1914. When war broke out, there was a call for volunteers to augment the regular army. In places the response was good, but in others there was some hesitation. In Accrington, a decision was taken to raise an infantry battalion of at least 600 men plus the ancillary troops such as signallers, machine gun cyclists and catering personnel. Recruitment was slow until the government adopted the idea of forming special battalions drawn from the same area or even from the same firm. This resulted in a surge of enlistment in early September 1914. Among the areas which responded to the call was Accrington, where a 'Pals' battalion was formed. The volunteers were placed under the command of retired NCOs and officers who proceeded to give the new recruits their basic training. Here volunteers are parading on Ellison Tenement. It has been suggested that the idea of regular employment did much to encourage men to enlist as it was a time of unemployment and poverty in the area. The picture shows that it was not only the working people who enlisted, but men from all walks of life.

Accrington 'Pals', 1914. Once the volunteers had enlisted, they were sent away to training camps in different parts of Lancashire for their basic training. Many of those from Accrington were sent after their initial training to Rugeley in Staffordshire, although the camp itself was on Cannock Chase.

Littleborough, *c.* 1914. When army battalions were at camp, for their training period, they stayed in tented villages similar to this one close to Hollingworth Lane between Littleborough and Milnrow.

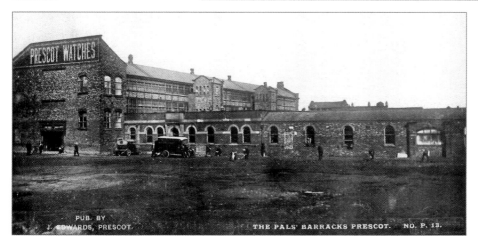

Prescot, 1914. Prescot Barracks came into existence at the outbreak of war in 1914. The buildings that became the barracks had been built in 1899 by the Lancashire Watch Company, which had closed in 1906. Several battalions raised in Liverpool were accommodated here as it was close to Knowsley Park where they trained.

Manchester, 1915. Although Manchester had several battalions of 'Pals' regiments, not all those from Manchester enlisted in these battalions. This photograph of May 1915 shows a large number of Manchester policemen who enlisted in the Grenadier Guards. Their police training would have enabled them to fit in to the rigid military regime more easily than many other volunteers.

Cleveleys, *c.* 1916. Which regiment these men were posted to and what they are doing is not clear, but all of the front row appear to be carrying rifles. It is possible that they were going on an exercise, perhaps to practice firing their rifles at a range somewhere on the coast.

Salford, 1918. Several shiploads of American troops arrived at Salford Docks on their way to the front. This photograph was taken when the first of the troops began to disembark; they were quickly moved to camps before being transferred to France and the front line.

Salford, 1915. The sinking of the liner *Luisitania* provoked an outbreak of rioting in many towns and cities against anyone who might be considered to have German connections. The easiest targets for the rioters to attack were shops where the name was clear for all to see. Here police are seen protecting damaged property from further destruction.

Bootle, 1918. The Mayor of Bootle is shown with two German guns captured by one of the battalions in the King's Liverpool Regiment. The guns would have been brought partially as a morale booster for the citizens at home, but also to show the bravery of local men.

45

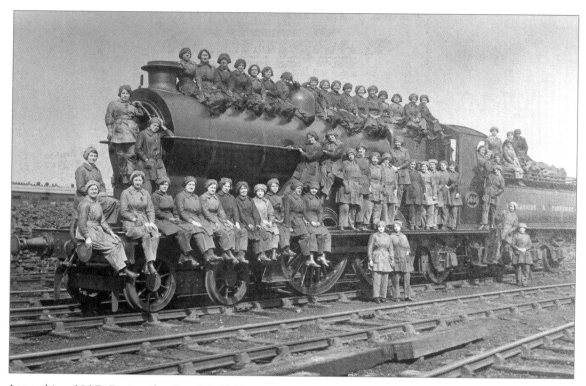

Lancashire, 1917. During the First World War many jobs were taken over by women. These women were employed by the Lancashire and Yorkshire Railway Company. They may have been cleaners at one of the company's locomotive depots or they may have been involved in production of engines at Horwich.

Skelmersdale, 1918. A group of women stand in front of a row of houses with their children. It is probable that this was a local shop and that the women had met up on their way to or from the shop.

Turton, 1914–18. Where is Turton on the photograph? The little white structures in the background are tents, which suggests that there was a large army camp in the area and that the gunpowder was being delivered there.

Leigh, *c.* 1918. With the end of the war, prisoners of war were exchanged and sent home. German prisoners of war march through Leigh, watched by large crowds. Even though the war was over, the Germans are under armed guard, not only to stop them escaping, but also to protect them from local people who might be hostile towards them.

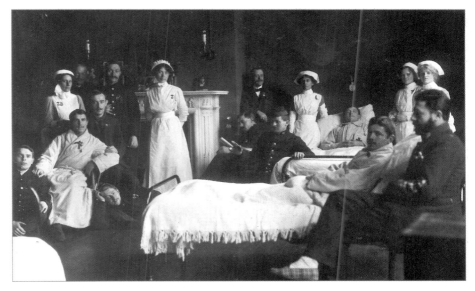

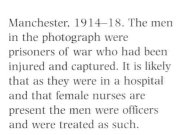

Manchester, 1914–18. The men in the photograph were prisoners of war who had been injured and captured. It is likely that as they were in a hospital and that female nurses are present the men were officers and were treated as such.

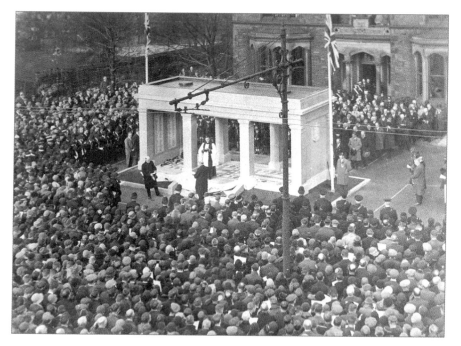

The War Memorial in Colne was dedicated on 11 November 1930. The Memorial was located on the main road in front of the Town Hall as a constant reminder of the sacrifices made by local people. On the side panels are inscribed the names of those from Colne who died in action or as a result of injuries received during the war.

Near Lancaster, *c.* 1926. The photograph shows troops marching away from either an Armistice Day service or the dedication of a war memorial in the 1920s as a large crowd look on.

Between the Wars

Astley Green, 1934. Opened in 1912, Astley Green Colliery soon became an important producer of coal, employing a large number of men. At the outbreak of war in 1939, this colliery employed 611 face workers, 701 other men underground and 471 surface workers, making a total of 1,783 people. When the pit was nationalised in the 1940s, it was employing 2,142 men of whom 1,584 worked underground. Here some of the men are leaving the pit head after coming to the surface at the end of a shift shortly after the ownership of the mine had passed to Manchester Collieries. Note the lack of protective hard hats which miners wear today, but they are carrying their safety lamps. The mine closed in 1970, but the no. 1 pit head gear and the winding house with its engine was retained and has become a landmark in the area, visible over long distances due to the flat nature of the land around it.

Leigh, 1938. One of the old ecclesiastical parishes of medieval Lancashire was centred on the small town of Leigh. The original church was demolished and replaced in 1870 by the one shown here. In front of the church, a marketplace developed, seen here with its stalls just before the outbreak of war in 1939. The obelisk among the canopies of the stalls is said to have been on the site of the original market cross.

Bacup, 1926. The view from Market Street looking towards its junction with Bridge Street. The hotel in the centre is the King George V Hotel which opened in 1912, replacing the Bull's Head Inn which had been demolished to enable Church Street (now Burnley Road) to be widened. It claimed to be the only hotel in the country to bear the name of a reigning monarch.

Nelson, *c.* 1929. The market hall was built in 1889 on the site of an older open air market. The clock tower was added in 1904, but the building was destroyed by fire in March 1932. The shop at the corner of Market Street and Scotland Road was Althams, a well known firm selling footwear.

Ashton-under-Lyne, *c.* 1919. Ashton-under-Lyne has its origins in the Middle Ages, being mentioned in the Domesday Book. This is Old Square, which was formed at the junction of Grey Street and George Street. Old Square, together with Stamford Street, formed the main shopping street of the town.

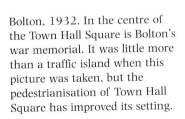

Crawshawbooth, *c.* 1930. Houses and public buildings cling to the steep hillsides while the flatter land is used for industrial purposes. The large church in the foreground is a non-conformist chapel, of which there were two in the village, one a Baptist Chapel and the other a Primitive Methodist Chapel.

Bolton, 1932. In the centre of the Town Hall Square is Bolton's war memorial. It was little more than a traffic island when this picture was taken, but the pedestrianisation of Town Hall Square has improved its setting.

Preston, *c.* 1925. One of the main streets of central Preston is Fishergate, the lower part of which is dominated by the Baptist Church designed by James Hibbert and built between 1858 and 1859. Next to the church, on the extreme left of the picture, is Loxham's motor car showroom. This building appears to have been adapted from another building on the site. Its roof has been taken off and a flat roof added whilst the first floor over the window has been strengthened so that cars can also be displayed on the upper floor. Across the road from the church is the Theatre Royal, which was built on the site of a former theatre, opened in 1802 in readiness for the Preston Guild of that year. The theatre was closed and demolished in the 1950s and replaced by a cinema, which has now also closed. The tower in the background is that of Preston Town Hall. The splendid building was designed by Sir Giles Gilbert Scott and opened in 1862. Unfortunately, a fire in 1947 resulted in its destruction and subsequent demolition.

MUMPS.

"OWDHA

TOMMYFIELD.

OLDH
No 43

CURZON STREET,

STAR INN.

Oldham, *c.* 1923. Interesting views and places in and around Oldham. Each mill and factory had its own steam engine for which a chimney was required. The central picture shows the view that travellers by train from Manchester would have had as they approached the town by train up the Werneth Incline. Tommyfield Market (bottom left) was Oldham's main market. Oldham Mumps (top left), is the railway bridge that carried the line from Manchester to Rochdale via Oldham. The top right shows one of Oldham's main shopping streets, Curzon Street, packed with shoppers who appear to be oblivious to traffic.

Nelson, *c.* 1937. In the 1920s and 1930s, the usual way to travel to the seaside was by train. During wakes weeks, special trains were run from Lancashire's cotton towns to the coast to move the large number of people who wanted to get to places like Southport, Blackpool and Morecambe.

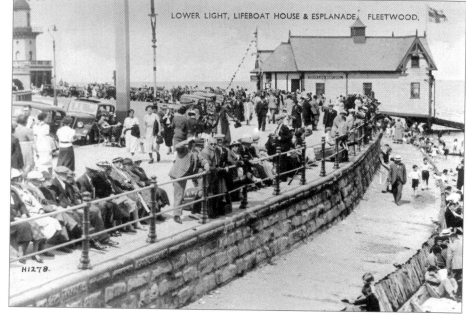

Fleetwood, *c.* 1935. Fleetwood became a popular destination for trippers from east Lancashire until Blackpool was connected to the railway. Although Blackpool became the most popular of the holiday resorts on the Flyde coast, Fleetwood also developed its own holiday industry as well as becoming an important fishing port and ferry terminal.

Knott End, *c.* 1938. In 1934, the London, Midland and Scottish Railway reluctantly decided to enter the holiday accommodation market by converting railway coaches, destined to be broken up, into 'caravans' or, as they were later known, 'camping coaches'. These coaches were located at popular holiday resorts such as Blackpool and Knott End.

Ainsdale, c. 1930. Some of the miles of sand dunes around Southport have been turned into golf courses as at Birkdale, but there is still sufficient room for members of the public to enjoy the sandy beaches. This appears to be an organised camp, but it is not clear for whom it was erected.

Southport, 1921–2. An effect of the receding of the sea was that large expanses of sand were exposed throughout the day, only being covered by the occasional exceptional tide. Here a high tide at Southport has attracted the interest of many onlookers.

St Anne's-on-Sea, 1920. The development of St Anne's started in 1875. By 1885 the decision had been taken to erect a pier to which a pavilion was added in 1899 and a Floral Hall in 1910. This postcard of the pier was posted in September 1920.

Blackpool, *c.* 1928. Until 1928, the Blackpool skyline was dominated by two man-made structures, the Tower, completed in 1894, and the Big Wheel, finished in 1896. These two tourist attractions, coupled with the amusement park, turned Blackpool into the north-west's premier holiday resort, attracting hundreds of thousands of visitors each year during the summer months. Apart from the Tower and the Big Wheel, the beach was probably the most favoured place for visitors, especially with young children, who could play safely on the sands and in the water. This photograph, taken just before the closure and demolition of the wheel, shows how crowded the beach could become not only with humans, but also donkeys and stalls. Behind the beach, the promenade also looks very crowded with the trams making their way along the front from the pleasure beach to Fleetwood.

Blackpool, 1939. A group of visitors to Blackpool appear to be engrossed in the game in progress at either the Pleasure Beach or at one of the many amusement places along the promenade.

Blackpool, *c.* 1935. Crowds line the promenade at Blackpool for what may have been the Blackpool Carnival Procession, which was held in the height of summer when there would have been many visitors in the town. The float at the back of the procession appears to be showing different periods of bathing costumes and the type of bathing machine which was used. During the early nineteenth century, men and women were not allowed to bathe together. At some places, men seen spying on ladies bathing were fined a bottle of wine!

Blackpool, *c.* 1930. The first illuminations were put on in Blackpool when five tram cars, which were powered by electricity, travelled up and down the front to mark Queen Victoria's Golden Jubilee. It was not until 1912 that illuminations similar to those which are seen today began to attract visitors.

Wigan, 1932. Were it not for the electric lights, it would be easy to imagine that this photograph had been taken in the latter half of the nineteenth century. It was actually taken in December 1932 at one of the collieries owned by the Wigan Coal and Iron Company. The women are working at the pit head grading coal and taking out lumps of stone and earth which had found their way, either accidentally or deliberately, into the tubs which were hoisted to the surface. The men working underground sometimes deliberately put in lumps of soil and rock to increase the weight and fill the tubs faster, thus increasing their wages as they would have been paid by the tub load. The work the women were doing was very dirty and cut their hands terribly. The scarves they wore were wound tightly round their heads to reduce the amount of dust that got into their hair and onto their clothes.

The cotton industry, *c.* 1930. The interior of a cotton mill in Lancashire during the inter-war years where the women are winding cotton yarn from cops onto reels. It was labour-intensive, as can be seen by the number of girls at each machine. Although the floor looks clean, the atmosphere within the room would have been dusty.

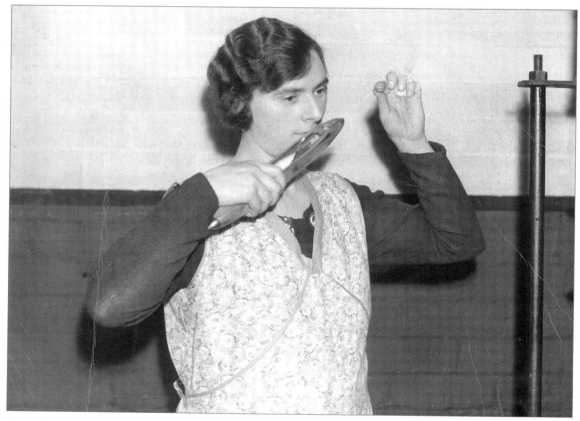

Lancashire, *c.* 1925. 'Kissing the shuttle' is carried out by a weaver threading the end of the thread through a small hole at the end of the shuttle. Doing this regularly caused cancer of the lips, due to the various oils and greases used in the cotton weaving and spinning processes.

Fleetwood, *c. 1930*. This photograph shows the Wyre dock at Fleetwood, built around 1878, with some of the many fishing boats tied up. Behind the fishing boats are fish packing sheds, which had railway connections so that the fish could be moved quickly to the markets. In the foreground are three larger general cargo vessels.

600 H.P. Thames Steam Tug "Blue Circle"

Lytham, *c. 1935*. Few people realised that Lytham had a small ship building industry which specialised in tugs and 'stern wheelers'. Among the vessels constructed there was the *Luggard* which appeared as *The African Queen* in the film of the same name. The shipyards were involved in the construction of the Mulberry Harbour used after the Normandy landings in 1944. The shipyards closed in 1955. The tug shown here was built for service on the River Thames.

Barrow-in-Furness, *c. 1935*. The Devonshire Dock was a large expanse of water, protected from the rise and fall of the tide by a dock gate. It was adjacent to the Walney Channel, into which ships were launched. On the opposite side of the basin can be seen extensive railway marshalling yards which originally belonged to the Furness Railway. The shipyards made vessels for both the Royal Navy and the Merchant Navy.

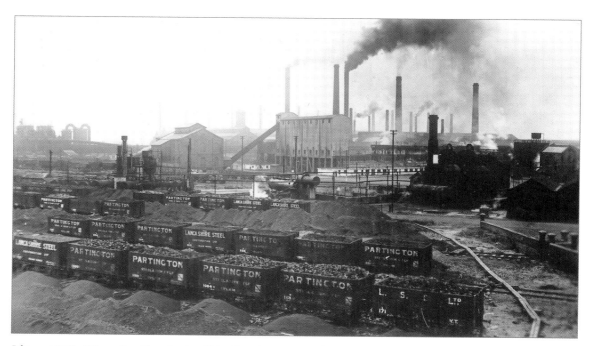

Irlam, 1920. When the Manchester Ship Canal was opened, new industries established themselves along its banks on former agricultural land. One of these firms was the Lancashire Steel company which built a large steel works at Irlam. The canal was used to bring in the raw materials as well as transport the finished products to their destinations. This picture shows the steel works and the extensive coal sidings at Irlam which were required for the blast furnaces. In the background are some of the buildings used to produce the steel. Working inside the steel works was a hot, dirty and dangerous occupation with molten metal everywhere.

Irlam, c. 1934. Molten iron or steel is being drawn off from the furnace and channeled into wagons under the staging. It looks as if one wagon has already been filled and that one of the men is busy blocking off the channel to stop the molten metal flowing into it, having already built a dam to divert it into an empty wagon.

Rossendale, 1927. One of the main employments in the Rossendale valley between the wars was the manufacture of slippers and sandals. It is said that the founder of the Rossendale footwear industry was J.W. Rothwell who started a factory in Waterfoot in 1874 using felt, which was an off-shoot of the woollen industry. Slippers had been made for many years before Rothwell established his factory by those working in the woollen industry who used to wrap waste felt around their feet to prevent cloth being damaged by their clogs. In the early part of the twentieth century the factory, owned by H.W. Trickett, was employing over 1,000 people and turning out 72,000 pairs of slippers a month in a former cotton mill. By 1927 between 6,000 and 7,000 people were employed in the Rossendale slipper industry.

Chorley, c. 1938. Although the eastern and southern fringes of Lancashire tended to be industrial in nature and the western edge devoted to the holiday industry, much of the central area was rural, with agriculture playing an important part in the economy.

Preston, 1922. Preston Guild is held every twenty years to mark the granting of a Guild Charter in 1179 by Henry II, which allowed the town to have a 'Guild Merchant with all its liberties and free customs'. The Guild consists of a number of processions through the centre of the town, together with church services and the reading of the charter.

Widnes, 1925. Between the wars, members of the Royal family frequently visited Lancashire. Such visits always attracted large crowds of spectators who lined the route. This photograph shows some of the people who were present as the Mayor welcomed King George V to Widnes.

Aintree, 1935. The Grand National has been run at Aintree Racecourse since 1839. 'Reynoldstown', shown here, won consecutive Grand Nationals in 1935 and 1936, a feat not repeated until 1973 and 1974 when 'Red Rum' did the same.

Rochdale, 1939. This photograph was taken during a cup tie between Salford and Wigan at the ground of Rochdale Hornets, the home of Rochdale Rugby League Club. One of the stands collapsed, causing serious injury to a number of spectators.

South Lancashire, 1934. When King George V visited the north west in 1934, he not only laid the foundation stone for the extension to Manchester Town Hall and officially opened the new Central Library, he also opened the East Lancashire Road. This dual carriage road was built to relieve traffic congestion in towns and villages between Manchester and Liverpool and to provide a quicker route between the two cities. The new road did not continue into the city centres but ended on the outskirts, reducing the benefits of faster travel which the road itself brought.

Liverpool, 1935. The Mersey Tunnel began in the centre of Liverpool, close to the docks, and ran for 2.13 miles under the river to Birkenhead. The tunnel, which cost over £7 million, was officially opened by King George V in July 1934.

Preston, *c.* 1925. Although Preston stands on the navigable stretch of the River Ribble, it had not been a significant port. In order to change that, Preston Council purchased forty acres of land and transformed them into the 'largest single dock basin in the world', which was opened in 1892. This photograph shows how much of the quay side was unused at the time. In the background, mill and factory chimneys belch out black smoke. In 1914, the docks at Preston handled almost ¾ million tons of goods, but by 1919 this had declined to just over 150,000 tons. By 1940, it was back up to more than 900,000 tons. However, with larger ships and changing export markets, the docks gradually declined and were eventually closed in the 1970s.

Barton, 1931. During the 1920s and 1930s, several aerodromes were opened in Lancashire, although it was not until 1929 that the first municipally owned airfield was opened, at Rackhouse, Manchester, then transferred to Barton until 1938. Here, Frances Day, an actress of some repute in the 1930s, poses at Barton Aerodrome.

Pendlebury, 1926. Safety men at Pendlebury Colliery stoke the boilers to keep the pumps working during the general strike. If these had ceased operating, the mine would have flooded and any return to work delayed or made impossible.

Lancashire contingent on its way to London, 1936. The man at the front appears to be carrying a collecting box for donations towards costs incurred during the march. Apparently, the route took the men through 'friendly' areas where they were often given food and accommodation for the night.

Nelson, 1936. This protest march shows the strength of support for weavers who were protesting about the cuts in wages that were being implemented by employers. Wage cuts were one way in which the employers tried to reduce costs in the face of foreign competition in the 1920s and '30s. A few years earlier they had also met with Ghandi in an attempt to reduce what the employers regarded as unfair competition from India where wages were much lower.

During the 1930s, various schemes were implemented to occupy those who were unemployed. Special centres were established to ensure that men, accustomed to working every day, had something to do with their time.

The top left photograph shows men at an unemployed centre, possibly in Bolton, playing draughts. The top right picture is of young men attending a camp at Ulveston in 1939 organised by the Lancashire and Cheshire Community Council, where they are being shown how to throw a javelin. This camp had replaced ones at Bowness and at Edale.

The bottom left was taken in 1934 when unemployed men were given the job of planting raspberries at Upholland, between Wigan and Ormskirk. The final photograph, which comes from the 1920s, shows how those living in the mining areas managed to get coal by scavenging the local slag heaps, a dangerous and dirty job, but it did provide fuel for heating their homes.

These pictures show how entertainment evolved during the 1920s and 1930s: top, a carnival in Darwen involving a number of floats; bottom left, a 'wireless discussion group' in Leigh Library, 1930 – a programme would be listened to and then discussed; bottom right, the local picture house in Colne.

Salford, 1929. Children playing in the streets were a common sight in towns and villages throughout Lancashire. Here, in Cleminson Street, one of the children appears to have been given a toy car, which has encouraged the other children of the neighbourhood to be photographed with it. It is interesting to see two of the boys rather proudly wearing their school uniform.

Barrowford, 1923. This photograph shows pupils from Year 3 of a local school in the costumes they wore to mark May Day. In the centre is Jessie Metcalfe, who was May Queen that year, and the others are presumably her attendants. The Year 2 children danced round the maypole on this occasion.

Rishton, 1937. The coronation of George VI was the first to be broadcast on the new medium of the wireless, which an increasing number of people could now afford. However, this did not stop local celebrations taking place with bands playing in parks, street parties and momentoes for school children.

Horwich, 1937. This factory was decorated for the coronation of George VI. The firm was perhaps involved in the bleaching or dyeing industry, with this part of the factory used for inspecting and folding cloth.

The Second World War

Manchester, 1939. In Manchester, like all large cities, plans were made to evacuate all the school children and expectant mothers to areas that were regarded as relatively safe from attack by the German airforce. Some Manchester children were evacuated to Lancashire, although many were sent to Cheshire, Staffordshire and Shropshire.

Nelson, 1930s. During the 1930s, groups of pacifists developed who were opposed to war, but equally opposed to what the Nazis in Germany stood for. This group entered a float in a gala procession organised by Reedymere Hospital at Nelson. The lady standing on the right of the banner is Mrs J. Cooper, JP, a former suffragette.

Eccles, 1939. As the outbreak of war approached, preparations were made to provide public air raid shelters in areas where the public might congregate, such as shopping centres or bus stations. These men were digging up a plot of unused land at the side of Silk Street in Eccles.

Chorley, 1939. As well as air raid shelters, trenches were also dug in town centres and other places where people might congregate. Although they would not have provided as much protection as air raid shelters, they would have protected people from the effects of the blast. These trenches are being dug in Chorley, which was regarded as a relatively safe area as there were no major industrial plants nearby.

Anderson shelters, 1939. Anderson shelters were built by householders in their gardens by digging a large trench and then erecting the corrugated iron sheets over it to provide a cover. Earth or sandbags were placed over the shelter to provide added protection. Some who covered their shelter with earth used the roof to grow vegetables.

Preston, *c.* 1939. Local authorities sandbagged public buildings as protection from blast damage. Behind the sandbags were often large windows which, if broken by a blast, could cause serious injury.

Manchester, 1939. When war broke out in September 1939, it was obligatory for everyone to carry a gas mask and to know how to use one. These small boys in Manchester appear to be being taught how to put them on correctly.

Lancaster, 1939–40. Lancaster was an important military centre, with the King's Own Royal Regiment (Lancaster) based at Bowerham Barracks. In the photographs above, the Mayor of Lancaster is visiting the barracks. In the bottom picture, locals are providing troops with what might be called 'home comforts' – a cup of tea, cakes and pies.

Accrington, 1940. In June 1940, the first bombs fell on the Lancashire town of Accrington, although the newspapers at the time reported that it was 'a town in the north west'. Why the stick of bombs was dropped has never been explained but it destroyed a house, killing a woman and her daughter outright, and severely injuring the husband who had to have his foot amputated. He died shortly afterwards in hospital. The son, who was at the back of the house, escaped virtually uninjured. After the war, the house was never rebuilt, but was turned into a memorial garden to the three who were so tragically killed. Since the war, it has been learned that, until a short time before the bombing, the couple had provided a home to two evacuees from Leeds, sent to Accrington because it was regarded as a safe place. The younger of the two evacuee sisters involved would not settle and the children returned home, having escaped death by a matter of days. This photograph shows the damaged house and those who came to look at it. Further along the road, another of the bombs created a large crater in a garden. It was said that this was the first air raid on Lancashire and that the three who died were the first victims of air attack in the county.

Wigan, *c.* 1940. Rationing was introduced so that everyone theoretically had the same. Ration books were issued and these had to be taken to the shop where the customer was registered. Rationing did not only apply to food, it also applied to clothing and even things like sweets and cigarettes.

Rochdale, 1941. During the war, parks and other unused land were handed over to gardeners who converted them into allotments and grew food there. Even playing fields were dug up and householders dug up their flower beds and planted vegetables so the basic food rations could be increased.

Although Manchester and Liverpool bore the brunt of the bombing in 1940, surrounding areas also suffered: top left, damage to buildings on the Crescent in Salford during the so-called Christmas raid on Manchester in December 1940; top right, Old Trafford Police Station. Although industrial areas were prime targets during the war, bombs and land mines also landed in more rural areas, where they were least expected. The photograph below shows members of the AFS inspecting a parachute that dropped a land mine near an air raid shelter in Adlington.

Weaste, 1941. Those who were too old to be called up, unfit, or in reserved occupations could join the Local Defence Volunteers (LDF), later known as the Home Guard. When first formed, the men had neither uniforms nor guns. Gradually this changed and members were properly equipped and trained. These men are being taught to use a rifle.

Accrington, 1942. This photograph shows the laboratory at the Broad Oak Print Works where John Whitford and J.T. Dickson discovered Terylene.

Blackpool, 1940. People on holiday enjoying the autumn sunshine. There is nothing to indicate that the country was at war when this photograph was taken in September 1940.

Blackpool, c. 1944. Posted in September 1944, this postcard was certainly of pre-war vintage and may have been produced as an advertising postcard for guests staying at the Crescent Hotel.

Manchester on VE Day, 6 May 1945. This scene was taken when the war in Europe ended. Large crowds roamed the streets of the centre of Manchester celebrating the return of peace in Europe. However, it was another three months before the Japanese surrendered, a surrender which was received with even greater joy in Manchester as there were many men from the north-west fighting in the Far East. This crowd of merry makers were in Mount Street, passing the Friends Meeting House and Central Library, but where they were heading is not known.

The Postwar Years

Accrington, 1953. The Coronation of Queen Elizabeth II provided an opportunity for everyone to enjoy themselves. In Accrington, a carnival procession was held on Saturday 6 June which was watched by over 50,000 people. Various local firms and organisations entered floats, which are seen here approaching the Town Hall.

Salford, 1950. When Ewan McColl wrote the song 'Dirty old town' in the 1950s, he was writing about Salford with its densely packed streets of houses and the factories close by. During the 1950s, clearance areas were designated and scenes like this gradually became things of the past. When these areas were cleared, it is said that in moving people out, the spirit of community that had existed was destroyed.

Salford, 1953. The death of George VI in February 1952 and the accession of Elizabeth II in 1953 ushered in a period of optimism. Local authorities decorated the streets and squares of town and city centres, and local people decorated the streets where they lived, holding street parties similar to this one in Barraclough Street, Salford.

Accrington, 1953. On 31 May, twelve churches joined together to hold a service in Oak Hill Park at Accrington. The procession, which started at Broadway, was ½ mile long and did not involve either the Church of England or the Roman Catholic churches in the town. When the procession reached the park, a service was held and prayers said for the new Queen. This photograph shows some of the congregation who attended that service, where singing was accompanied by the Salvation Army band.

Oldham, *c.* 1950. This photograph, in the late 1940s or early 1950s, shows a queue of women and children entering a building, possibly to collect their ration books. It was only very gradually that restrictions were relaxed and goods became more freely available.

Southport, *c.* 1950. The arrival of the private motor car and its effect on towns is clearly illustrated by this picture of Lord Street in Southport as every possible parking spot has been taken. However, at this point in time, it was still the train and bus which brought many visitors to Lancashire's seaside resorts.

Wigan, *c.* 1958. All Saints church, in the background, was the centre of an extensive parish comprising fourteen townships in the West Derby Hundred, and it had been rebuilt and enlarged several times. Other buildings in the photograph include the post office, on the extreme left, a hotel and a bank, on the right.

Rawtenstall, *c.* 1950. One of the most important towns of the Rossendale Valley is Rawtenstall which developed as a textile town in the 1950s taking advantage of the River Irwell and its tributaries. It is now the terminus of the East Lancashire Railway. The building on the left is the entrance to Rawtenstall Goods Depot.

Salford, *c.* 1960. The clearance of areas of poor-quality housing transformed towns and cities in the two decades after the Second World War. This photograph shows the effect of slum clearance programmes on the Regent Road area in Salford. Many of the terraced houses have disappeared but in their place are caravans possibly associated with those involved with travelling fairs.

Mosley Common, *c.* 1959. The first shaft was sunk at Mosley Common in 1868 and this was followed by four others over the next twenty years. Here, railway wagons filled with coal are sorted and made into trains before being sent to the main line and onwards to various parts of the country. Mosley Common colliery eventually closed in 1968 and all trace of its existence on the surface has been removed.

Salford, *c.* 1959. Although known as Manchester Docks, the largest of the docks on the Manchester Ship Canal were to be found in Salford. Traffic using the canal continued to increase, with the docks at the Manchester and Salford end remaining busy into the 1960s. By the early 1980s, only a few ships were using the full length of the canal and the decision was taken to close the docks and redevelop the area.

Leyland, 1998. Although this photograph was taken in 1998, the vehicle in the picture was built in Lancashire by Leyland in 1946, when it was known as a Leyland Beaver. It was customised for a Yorkshire brewery to deliver barrelled beer to local public houses and hotels.

Bolton, 1950. Three forms of transport feature on this photograph taken under the Bradford Street Bridge in Bolton: the Manchester, Bolton and Bury canal, the railway bridge which carried the line from Bolton towards Darwen and Blackburn, and the lorries which are bringing in the rubbish to fill in the canal.

In 1948, two Lancashire clubs faced each other in the Cup Final at Wembley – Blackpool and Manchester United. Here, United captain, Johnny Carey, introduces the team to King George VI. United won the match 4–2, their first FA Cup win since they beat Bristol City in 1909. Five years later, Blackpool went on to win the cup after a thrilling final against Bolton Wanderers.

Chadderton, 1954. Members of the Rochdale Hounds at Chadderton Fold appear to be on foot rather than horseback so it may have been a drag hunt rather than a hunt for foxes.

Wigan, 1948. During a local by-election, Labour candidate, Mr R. Williams, stopped to talk to a lady, Mrs Kenny, leaving a local fish and chip shop. According to the information on the reverse of the photograph, Mr Williams asked Mrs Kenny what she was carrying in her basins and was told that they contained fish and chip dinners for her family of eight people. In the window is an advertisement for one of Lancashire's best known pie makers, Hollands, who are still in business today.

The 1960s and 1970s

Radcliffe, *c.* 1965. An important part of many of Lancashire's towns is the local market. Some markets are covered and the traders protected from the weather, while others are the more traditional market stalls that are erected and taken down each market day.

Radcliffe, 1961. This is Market Place, Radcliffe, looking towards the viaduct, that carried the railway from Clifton Junction to Bury and Rawtenstall, and Radcliffe Bridge Station, which closed in 1959. In the foreground is the old market hall and the market place, which was being used as a bus station.

Audenshaw, *c.* 1965. In 1974, a number of small urban district councils and municipal boroughs around the east edge of Manchester were absorbed by either Oldham or Tameside Metropolitan Borough Councils. One of these was Audenshaw which lay between Manchester and Ashton-under-Lyne and became part of Tameside Metropolitan Borough. The proximity of Audenshaw to both Manchester and Ashton-under-Lyne and the existence of good public road transport, in the form of both buses and trolley buses, meant that the area developed a residential character as several of the photographs on this postcard show.

Little Hulton, *c.* 1970. During the 1960s and 1970s, new shopping centres were developed in areas to which people were moving. As the age of the car was dawning, it is interesting to note that when the centre was planned provision had been made for only limited car parking.

Ashton-in-Makerfield, near Wigan, *c.* 1961. The chimney and the pit head gear were familiar features in this part of Lancashire until the gradual decline of heavy industry. Surrounding the mills, factories and mines were rows of terraced houses, built originally for local workers.

Ashton-in-Makerfield, *c.* 1961. This view shows the type of housing that existed in the industrial towns and villages of Lancashire into the mid-twentieth century. These houses were erected in the nineteenth century for workers in local factories, mines and mills so that they did not have a long walk to work.

South-west Lancashire, *c.* 1961. The farmland in the Bickerstaff area was, and still is, used for growing crops such as potatoes, carrots, cauliflowers and other vegetables which found ready markets in the towns and cities of Lancashire as well as further afield.

South-east Lancashire, *c.* 1961. Another section of Lancashire's greenbelt lies between Kearsley and Walkden in south-east Lancashire. In the background are several cotton mills and their associated chimneys and the occasional church tower. Some of the land does not appear to be used for agricultural purposes, but left in its natural state.

Milnrow, 1963. One topic of conversation when people meet is the weather and the winter of 1962/3 was certainly cause for comment. Several weeks of snow, ice and temperatures about or below freezing caused Hollingworth Lake, in the foreground, to freeze over.

Bolton, c. 1959. Fishing has always been a popular pastime. These three boys are fishing in the lake of a Bolton park. Only one of them appears to have a proper fishing rod.

Horwich, 1965. This line was opened in 1870, and achieved importance in the 1880s when the decision was made to build a new locomotive works in Horwich to replace the existing works at Miles Platting and Bury. This photograph shows a Stanier 2-6-4 tank locomotive, based at Bolton, about to depart for Blackrod, thus ending ninety-five years of passenger traffic on the line.

Widnes, 1961. Opened by Princess Alexandra of Kent in 1961, the new Runcorn–Widnes Bridge enabled faster and more convenient communication between the north and south banks of the Ship Canal and Mersey for road vehicles and replaced the transporter bridge

THE DOCKS, HEYSHAM

S. 894

Heysham, *c.* 1965. With its proximity to Ireland and the Isle of Man, it was natural that ports would develop in Lancashire to provide direct communications to both countries. In order to meet the growing demand for transport across the Irish Sea, and to provided a deep water port which was accessible 24 hours a day without the need for lock gates, the port of Heysham was developed. Construction of Heysham Docks took seven years and involved the use of 2,000 navvies, who lived in special villages near the construction site. Gradually the port developed so that, by the outbreak of war in 1939, there were five daily sailings from Heysham to Ireland, the evening sailing being served by 'The Ulster Express', which left London Euston around 6 p.m. One of the ferries for Ireland can be seen moored in the background. Heysham was, and still is, an important ferry terminal. The presence of a freighter in the foreground also indicated the importance of the deep water port for vessels carrying freight. More recently, the development of the gas fields in Morecambe Bay has seen new types of traffic using the port, serving the oil and gas rigs out at sea.

Barton, *c.* 1979. In 1960, the Stretford–Eccles bypass was opened, reducing congestion in a large part of the west of Manchester. The construction of the new road resulted in the need to build a new crossing of the River Mersey at Dumplington, which became known as Barton High Level Bridge. The Stretford–Eccles by-pass became the first link in the Manchester outer ring road, whose completion date is given as 'Summer 2000'. This photograph, taken by archaeologists, shows the Manchester Ship Canal and the Barton High Level Bridge shortly before the bridge was widened to take an extra lane of traffic in each direction. In the foreground is the Davyhulme Sewage Works, which was built by Manchester City Council in the late nineteenth century to treat sewage before discharging it into the Manchester Ship Canal. Later specially designed sludge boats were introduced to carry the sewage into Liverpool Bay. The area where these boats were loaded is clearly shown on the photograph, close to Barton Lock. Both the large and the small locks are visible together with the sluice gates which were used to regulate the level of the water in the canal and ensure that the surrounding areas were not submerged in times of heavy rain. Beyond the high level bridge is Barton Road Bridge, which was constructed in 1893 when the Manchester Ship Canal was built, and the Barton Swing Aqueduct on the Bridgewater Canal, which appears to be in the 'open' position to allow vessels to use the Ship Canal.

Accrington, *c.* 1961. Although the date on the back of this photograph of Accrington Stanley FC is given as 19–29 July 1961, the season did not start until the middle of August 1961 according to the local papers. The only pre-season friendly played was against Stockport County the previous week. Accrington Stanley, or Accrington FC, was formed *c.* 1876 and joined the Football League when it was set up in 1888. However, the club resigned from the League in 1892 when the Second Division was formed. Accrington FC did not survive into the twentieth century, support declined for the old club and eventually it was dissolved. However another team in the town, Stanley Villa, was receiving a lot of support and eventually this became Accrington Stanley FC, which rejoined the Football League in 1921. During the next forty years, the club had mixed fortunes, rising to second place in Division 3 (North) in the 1954/5 season. This was the highest position the club ever reached. Gradually, support for the club declined, and financial difficulties followed. By February 1962, the club owed £62,000 and it was threatened that the water, gas and electricity would be cut off and the players would go unpaid. The decision was taken to resign from the Football League, the letter of resignation being accepted on 11 March 1962. For the record, Accrington Stanley lost its last game in the Football League 4–0 to Crewe. The club itself was wound up and ceased to exist in 1966 although another club with the same name was formed two years later and still plays today, but in the Unibond League. When this photograph was taken, the club appears to have a lot of support, but was it a cup match and if so when?

Modern Lancashire

On 20 December 1984, a train of thirteen petrol wagons derailed and caught fire in Summit Tunnel, between Littleborough and Todmorden. Flames from the ventilation shafts forced the evacuation of fire fighters and people who lived and worked nearby in case a fireball burst out of the tunnel entrances. It was three days before British Rail engineers could enter the tunnel to inspect the damage done by the fire.

Warrington, 1998. At the end of August 1998, the Inland Waterways Association held its annual rally at Salford Quays. Although many narrow boats and canal cruisers made their way to Salford along the Bridgewater Canal, the highlight for many boat owners was the opportunity to sail along the Manchester Ship Canal in their own boats for the first time. This photograph, taken at Warrington as the convoy passed the Chester Road Bridge, shows what has been described as the largest convoy ever to sail along the Ship Canal. In the background is Acton Grange Bridge, which carries the West Coast main line. As the boats in the convoy had been designed to sail under fixed bridges with little headroom, there was no need to swing the road bridges much to the relief of motorists who would otherwise have been held up. Normally, small craft are not allowed on the Ship Canal because of the dangers of being run down by ocean going ships. When the convoy passed through the locks, each capable of taking a 12,000 ton container ship, almost all those taking part could be accommodated in a single operation. Even on this occasion, the convoy was escorted by pilot vessels to ensure that all went smoothly and to warn the crews of dangers or tricky conditions, especially east of Warrington where the River Mersey crosses the Ship Canal. A similar trip along the Manchester Ship Canal was organised in June 2000 for vessels taking part in the IWA Manchester branch's Millennium Rally at Salford Quays. On this occasion, however, the small boats did not depart for home along the Ship Canal, but travelled to Hulme Lock and returned on canals which were more familiar with narrow boats and cruisers.

St Helens, 1987. The restoration of canals which had been allowed to fall into disrepair or which had been severed by modern motorway construction has been an important part of preserving Lancashire's industrial heritage.

One society, the Sankey Canal Restoration Society (SCARS), set about restoring the region's oldest artificial waterway, the Sankey Canal, which had been opened in 1752. One of the first jobs was to start clearing the locks at St Helens.

Work started in May 1986 using volunteers and very little equipment. By the following year (top), progress was being made and the lock walls and the location of the lock gates became clearly visible. It took another five years hard work by volunteers, and later by St Helen's Metropolitan Borough Council through a derelict land grant, to clear the lock and a quarter-mile of canal.

The new lock gates were fitted in September 1991 (middle) by which time the site had resumed the appearance of a canal with locks.

The official opening of the lock and restored section of canal took place in May 1992 when the SCARS trip boat *St Helens* took the Mayors of St Helens, Warrington and Widnes through the gates into the basin (bottom). SCARS is now continuing with its efforts to restore the whole length of the Sankey Canal to a navigable state.

Radcliffe, 1992. Another canal which had become unnavigable is the Manchester, Bolton and Bury Canal. Here several small boats use the canal at Radcliffe on a section which has been restored.

Salford, 1999. Since the Manchester, Bolton and Bury Canal Society was formed and the first section of the canal restored, further projects have been undertaken, sometimes in conjunction with other bodies. This photograph shows two boats on a restored section at Agecroft.

Liverpool and Rainhill, 1978 and 1980. The 150th anniversary, in 1980, of the opening of the world's first inter-city passenger railway service between Liverpool and Manchester caused industrial archaeologists and railway historians to take an interest in the line and what remained of the original structures: top, Edge Hill, Liverpool, and the tunnels that lead down to the docks – note the bases of two chimneys that appear on early engravings of the line; middle and bottom, a cavalcade of engines and rolling stock at Rainhill.

Milnrow, 1999. The Ellenroad Mill at Milnrow has been demolished, but the engine house remains. It houses several steam engines, together with the ones that drove the machinery in the mill. This is 'Phyllida', built in 1921 and used to provide lighting before the main engines were started up.

Tram Sunday in Fleetwood, 1999. On the third Sunday of July, thousands of people descend on the town to see in action the historic trams that have been restored and have the opportunity to ride on them.

Salford, 1989. During the latter half of the twentieth century, new shopping centres have been built in many towns, providing modern facilities, a wide range of shops, a good bus service and car parking.

Chorley, 2000. Although there has been some redevelopment in the centre of Chorley, it is on a relatively small scale when compared with that in other towns and has enabled the original main street to retain a variety of shops and financial institutions. Between the new development and the original main street is Chorley Market which, although not a lavish building, has a pleasant, friendly atmosphere and a wide range of goods on sale.

Blackburn, 2000. During the last forty years, Lancashire has developed into a multi-cultural and multi-ethnic society. The result has been the development of diverse yet vibrant communities.

Lancaster, 2000. Today, Lancaster is the mostly northerly of the cities and towns in Lancashire. Although it gave its name to the county, it is now the centre of a district council which includes former independent districts such as Morecambe and Heysham. The construction of the M6 motorway has provide some relief from the congestion which formerly blighted this town and enabled areas to be pedestrianised so that some of the fine buildings in the centre can be appreciated. The Castle is the oldest building in the city and for many years doubled as a prison, housing many well known, or notorious, prisoners such as the Pendle Witches. Today, it is a tourist attraction. During the nineteenth century Lancaster made its name through the presence of firms making linoleum and fine furniture. The wealth of these firms was gradually reflected in the new buildings that were erected in the late nineteenth and early twentieth centuries.

One of the largest out of town shopping centres was opened in 1998 in Dumplington, on the edge of Trafford Park. This huge shopping centre can be seen from quite a distance away with its bluey-green glass domes giving the whole complex an imposing appearance.

Salford, 2000. To commemorate the work of L.S. Lowry and provide a suitable home for its collection of paintings, Salford Art Gallery has built a new arts centre known as 'The Lowry' at the end of the former no. 9 Dock of Manchester docks.

Blackburn, 2000. A large part of the centre of Blackburn has been redeveloped. From the roof of the car park, it is possible to see how modern housing has replaced the old terraced housing on the hillsides. Closer to the centre, some of the older buildings have survived as offices and workshops.

Blackburn, 2000. Blackburn became the centre of an Anglican diocese in 1926, and the parish church of St Mary was elevated to the status of a cathedral at that time. The 1820s church was rebuilt after a fire in 1831. The original tower was retained and a tall, slender spire added in 1961.

Lancashire, 1999. Behind Horwich the Pennines rise sharply out of the Lancashire Plain to form what is now called the West Pennine Moors, centred on Rivington Pike. On a clear day, Blackpool Tower can be seen on the horizon, while Preston is hidden by a protruding ridge.

Horwich, 1999. From the top of Rivington Pike it is also possible to look down on part of the Greater Manchester conurbation at places like Horwich and Blackrod. The most obvious landmark from this position is the Reebok Stadium, built by Bolton Wanderers Football Club.

Blackpool, 1999. The end of 1999 and the beginning of 2000 was celebrated in different ways by different groups in the community. Plaques appeared outside most churches proclaiming the millennium while this illuminated sign was erected on the seafront at Blackpool.

Manchester, 1999. At the Castlefield Arena in Manchester, citizens of Manchester welcomed the new century and millennium with free entertainment and a firework display organised by the city council.

ACKNOWLEDGEMENTS AND PICTURE CREDITS

Compiling this selection of illustrations to show Lancashire in the twentieth century has been a challenge as so much material survives and so many different things have happened during the century.

My task has been made easier by the help I have received from many people, in particular: Catherine Duckworth at Accrington Library, Susan Halstead from Burnley Library, Mark Pearson from Littleborough Local History Society, Bernard and Gill Champness, David Taylor of Manchester Local Studies Unit, the Castlefield Visitor Centre in Manchester, Tim Ashworth from Salford Local History Library and all those who have contributed in some way, however small, to this book.

I wish to express my thanks to those librarians who were in charge of local studies collections in the early 1970s, when I was working on another book on Lancashire, who kindly allowed me access to their collections which enabled me to build up a nucleus of material on Lancashire. I should also like to thank Alan Godfrey for the reproductions of maps of various Lancashire towns at the beginning of the twentieth century which have proved to be so helpful in enabling streets and buildings to be located. The notes on the reverse of the maps also proved to be invaluable in providing information that is not easily obtainable elsewhere.

I would also like to thank the following people and organisations for permission to reproduce some of the photographs in this book including: Accrington Library, the Lancashire Libraries, Bernard and Gill Champness, Brian Proctor, Castlefield Visitor Centre, the Ellenroad Mill Trust, Colin and Cynthia Greenall and the Sankey Canal Restoration Society, John Fletcher and the Manchester, Bolton and Bury Canal Society, Andy Crossley of the Manchester branch of the Inland Waterways Association, Mrs J. Minshull, David Brearley and John Ryan, whose collections of postcards made looking for material so much easier.

Although I have tried to trace the owners of all those illustrations that required permission to reproduce, there are several for which there is no indication of ownership. I apologise for any infringement of copyright which might have occurred as a result of this failure and hope that the owners will accept this apology.

Special thanks must be given to David Brearley who has made copies of photographs for this book. Without David's help and assistance many of the illustrations in this book could not have been included. I must also thank Peter and Anna for their help and assistance and finally my wife, Hilary, for her help in reading drafts and making constructive suggestions about the content.